DOGS SET XI

Xoloitzcuintli

Kristin Petrie
ABDO Publishing Company

visit us at
www.abdopublishing.com

Published by ABDO Publishing Company, PO Box 398166, Minneapolis, MN 55439.
Copyright © 2014 by Abdo Consulting Group, Inc. International copyrights reserved
in all countries. No part of this book may be reproduced in any form without written
permission from the publisher. The Checkerboard Library™ is a trademark and logo of
ABDO Publishing Company.

Printed in the United States of America, North Mankato, Minnesota.
102013
012014
 PRINTED ON RECYCLED PAPER

Cover Photo: SuperStock
Interior Photos: Alamy pp. 7, 9; AP Images p. 11; Corbis pp. 13, 17, Glow Images pp. 5,
     19; iStockphoto pp. 15, 21

Editors: Tamara L. Britton, Megan M. Gunderson, Bridget O'Brien
Art Direction: Neil Klinepier

Library of Congress Cataloging-in-Publication Data

Petrie, Kristin, 1970-
  Xoloitzcuintli / Kristin Petrie.
     pages cm. -- (Dogs)
  Includes bibliographical references and index.
  ISBN 978-1-62403-104-5
1. Xoloitzcuintli--Juvenile literature. I. Title.
  SF429.X6.P48 2014
  636.76--dc23
                    2013028914

CONTENTS

THE DOG FAMILY

For many, a dog is a beloved family companion. Dogs gained their place in the lives of humans thousands of years ago. However, the first dogs were not companion animals. They were there to work.

Dogs are descendants of the gray wolf. Both animals are members of the family **Canidae**. Early humans tamed young wolves to help them hunt for food.

Over time, people recognized the dog's other useful qualities. They were soon put to use. Some **breeds** herded cattle. Others pulled sleds and hauled gear. Many became guard dogs.

Ancient American Indian groups believed one dog could guard against more than just **intruders**. This special dog is the rare and unusual Xoloitzcuintli (show-low-eetz-kweent-lee).

The Xoloitzcuintli

XOLOITZCUINTLI

The Xoloitzcuintli, or Xolo for short, is one of the world's oldest **breeds**. **Archaeologists** believe the Xolo's ancestors came to the Americas with humans who migrated from Asia across a frozen Bering Strait.

Artifacts found in Mexico show the Xolo has been there nearly 3,500 years. **Aztec** and other American Indian **cultures** believed the Xolo protected them from evil spirits. They also believed the Xolo had healing powers.

The breed was first recognized by the **American Kennel Club (AKC)** in 1887. However, it was so rare there were not enough dogs to create a breed standard. So in 1959, the Xolo lost its AKC recognition.

The Xoloitzcuintli Club of America formed in 1986 to save the **breed**. The club's hard work paid off. The Xolo regained its **AKC** recognition in 2011. Today, the number of Xolos is increasing. But the breed is still rare.

From 1887 to 1959, the Xoloitzcuintli was AKC recognized as the Mexican Hairless. Today, it is known by this name, too.

What They're Like

The adult Xolo is calm and attentive to its family. It often chooses one person as its favorite. But, it pays attention to others as well. Xolos are tolerant of children and other pets if raised with them from an early age.

The Xolo is a social **breed**. It loves to be involved in family activities. Its intelligence helps the Xolo to retain information and train well. However, this same intelligence helps the Xolo escape nearly any yard, cage, or room!

The Xolo is alert and territorial. It is an excellent guard dog. Since it does not bark often, any noise from the Xolo should alert owners to a disturbance.

The Xolo's name comes from the Aztec god Xolotl, and Itzcuintli, the Aztec word for dog.

The Xolo is a primitive **breed**. This means it lacks the long-term breeding that results in consistent characteristics. The Xolo may not be the best choice for first-time dog owners. But firm leadership, proper training, and **socialization** can make for a happy, well-behaved Xolo.

COAT AND COLOR

The Xolo is best known for its hairless body. Early Xolos had hair. Then, a genetic change resulted in hairless puppies. Today, there are both hairless and coated Xolos.

Coated Xolos are completely covered with short, smooth hair. In contrast, the hairless Xolo sprouts small tufts of hair on the top of its head, its toes, and the end of its tail!

Both types come in many colors. They range from black to red to bronze. Both may also have spots and other markings on their bodies.

The hairless Xolo's skin is smooth, tough, and fits snugly to the body. Being hairless is well

suited for the hot climate of the **breed**'s native land!
However, the lack of hair also exposes the Xolo
to heat and cold. So, they need sunscreen in the
summer and a sweater in the colder months.

Some people believe the Xolo's hairless body is hypoallergenic. Its lack of hair may cause fewer allergic reactions. But dander, saliva, and other allergens remain.

SIZE

The Xolo comes in three sizes. They are toy, miniature, and standard. Toy Xolos stand 10 to 14 inches (25 to 35 cm) at the shoulder. Miniature Xolos range from 14 to 18 inches (35 to 45 cm) in height. The standard Xolo runs from 18 to 23 inches (45 to 58 cm) tall. Because of their size differences, Xolos can weigh between 10 and 50 pounds (4.5 and 23 kg).

The Xolo holds its head high on a strong, graceful neck. The wedge-shaped skull has a long, tapered **muzzle**. High on the head, large erect ears taper to a rounded tip. The Xolo's almond-shaped eyes range in color from black to yellow.

The Xolo's body is lean and muscular. Long legs end in webbed paws that have arched toes. The tail is long, thin, and pointed. The Xolo is slightly longer than it is tall.

Many people dislike the Xolo's appearance with its hairless body, scanty Mohawk hairdo, and rat-like tail. But those who prize the **breed** appreciate its original looks.

The Xoloitzcuintli is the official dog of Mexico.

CARE

Like all dogs, the Xolo needs a good veterinarian. The vet can provide health exams and **vaccines**. He or she can also **spay** or **neuter** your dog.

It may seem that a hairless dog would not require grooming. While the hairless type does not need brushing, it does require care!

Hairless dogs will sometimes need a bath. Applying moisturizing lotion will keep the skin healthy. Some young Xolos may get **acne**. Don't pick at the bumps! Keeping the dog and its bedding clean will help with this problem.

The Xolo's nails grow quickly. They will need weekly trimming. A good time to do this is when caring for the dog's skin.

Don't forget regular dental care! Brushing the Xolo's teeth every day prevents gum disease and tooth decay. Begin care and grooming at an early age so these activities don't stress your Xolo.

The Xolo's skin produces an oil that protects it from the sun.

FEEDING

The Xolo is an active dog. So, it needs a high quality diet to supply energy. Protein, carbohydrates, fats, vitamins, and minerals provide for growth and immunity as well. Quality dog food provides these important **nutrients**.

Dog food comes in several kinds. These include moist, semimoist, and dry. Moist foods are easy for dogs to digest. They also contain some water, an important part of the Xolo's diet. Dry foods have a long shelf life. They can be left out without spoiling.

However, **breeders** recommend serving the Xolo scheduled meals. This helps prevent overeating and weight gain. Puppies need three or more small meals per day to support growth. Fully grown dogs

need one to two meals per day. Older and less active dogs need just a single meal each day. Don't forget to provide fresh water every day!

It is common for hairless Xolos to have missing teeth. But they still enjoy dinner and treats!

THINGS THEY NEED

The Xolo is an active dog. It needs a large area in which to run and play. But do not think a Xolo will stay put in a fenced yard! Leaping over a six-foot (2-m) fence is no problem for this athletic **breed**! So, be sure your dog has a sturdy collar and identification tags. A strong leash is also handy for long walks.

In addition to exercise, the Xolo needs the attention of its family. This may be in the form of play or simply snuggling. Early **socialization** and training will prevent unwanted behavior.

After playing and socializing, the Xolo may want to rest. A dog crate creates a safe, calm place for a tired Xolo. Crates are also ideal for travel and training.

The Xolo is a member of the AKC's non-sporting group.

PUPPIES

Like all dogs, the female Xolo is **pregnant** for about 63 days. After this time, a **litter** of four to five puppies is born. The litter can include both coated and hairless puppies.

Like all puppies, the tiny Xolos are born blind and deaf. They rely on their mother for everything. After two weeks, they can see and hear. At three weeks, the puppies take their first steps. Xolos that are twelve weeks old are ready for a new home.

Is a Xolo the right dog for your family? If so, look for a reputable **breeder**. It might take a while to find one, since Xolos are so rare.

Healthy Xolo puppies are very active. They need extra exercise and toys for chewing to avoid

culture - the customs, arts, and tools of a nation or a people at a certain time.

intruder - a person who enters a place without permission.

litter - all of the puppies born at one time to a mother dog.

muzzle - an animal's nose and jaws.

neuter (NOO-tuhr) - to remove a male animal's reproductive glands.

nutrient - a substance found in food and used in the body. It promotes growth, maintenance, and repair.

pregnant - having one or more babies growing within the body.

socialize - to adapt an animal to behaving properly around people or other animals in various settings.

spay - to remove a female animal's reproductive organs.

vaccine (vak-SEEN) - a shot given to prevent illness or disease.

WEB SITES

To learn more about Xoloitzcuintli, visit ABDO Publishing Company online. Web sites about Xoloitzcuintli are featured on our Book Links page. These links are routinely monitored and updated to provide the most current information available.

www.abdopublishing.com

INDEX